<u>Citations Made Simple:</u>

A Student's Guide to Easy Referencing

Vol. I: The APA Format

By Joanne M. Weselby

Licence Notes

Copyright: Joanne M. Weselby

Published: 13th September 2014

ISBN: 978-1502356420

CreateSpace Edition

Table of Contents

Introduction

As you move on from college and A-Levels to studying for a degree at University, you will notice that there are many more expectations placed upon you than there were before. One of the most important of these is the requirement for you to supply citations whenever you refer to a certain author or text.

So, for example, instead of writing "Freud argued that…", you will instead have to insert a short explanation of who the author is (if not mentioned already), when their work was published, and if you're quoting them directly, on what page those words appear in the version of the text you're using. This needs to be supplied each and every time you refer to an author or text.

The way in which you supply this information varies depending on which citation style your University prefers. There are many different variations, with some Universities having their own unique traditions in this regard, but of these, there are four variations which are most commonly used.

These common variations are:

- ❖ APA
- ❖ Harvard
- ❖ Chicago
- ❖ Vancouver

You probably haven't given this a lot of thought up until now, but referencing is actually really important at University: penalties are usually applied to the marks awarded to incorrectly formatted work, meaning that if you want to do well and obtain the highest grades, you'll need to become very familiar with the rules and requirements of your assigned citation format.

In order to help you to master this skill, this series of short guides will demonstrate how to use all of each four styles, by explaining the formatting differences between them, and showing you all the information you'll need to complete all your references correctly. We'll look at both in-text citation and bibliography listings, showing you how to reference books, journal and newspaper articles, chapters from edited volumes, and web sources, amongst others.

Are you ready to begin? Great, then let's get started!

General Requirements of APA Format

The 'APA' format (which stands for the American Psychological Association) is one of the most commonly used citation styles in both UK and US academic institutions. When using this format, citations should be supplied 'in-text' – that is, they should appear in the main body of your essay, directly after a particular author and/or text has been referred to.

As you may already be aware, there are several updates that have been implemented in the style guidelines for this format over the years (which is unsurprising, given that it was originally created in 1929), and so your academic institution will usually specify which version they would like you to use: e.g. APA (5th edition).

Please note that this book will outline the most recent version of the APA formatting guidelines – referred to as the 6th edition. If you are assigned an earlier version, there may be small variations to the required format than those outlined in this guide.

Work submitted in APA format should be typed and word-processed, presented on A4 (8.5" x 11") paper, with 1" margins on all sides. The document should be double-spaced throughout (excluding the bibliography), and presented in a clear, non-exotic font (Times New Roman, size 12 is usually the preferred format, although Arial, size 12 may also be acceptable).

Direct quotations that are forty words or longer should appear separately from the main body of the work, with quotation marks omitted, with a half-inch left indentation applied to the entire quote.

Additionally, APA (6th edition) formatting guidelines specify that a 'running head' (which is a page header containing a short version of the title of the work, which must not exceed 50 characters, written in capitals) should be included on every page. You also need to enter page numbers into this field, rather than inserting them at the bottom of the page. In an A4 document, this should all fit onto one line.

For example:

CITATIONS MADE SIMPLE   7

Please note that the first page's header should vary slightly to contain the full title of the work (again, all in capitals), preceded by the words 'Running Head' (not capitalised). Again, ideally, in an A4 document, this would all fit onto one line.

For example:

Running Head: CITATIONS MADE SIMPLE: A STUDENT'S GUIDE TO EASY REFERENCING   1

You will be expected to supply a bibliography listing all the work you have referred to when completing your essay, which should be inserted after the main body of the text on a fresh page (more on this later).

Finally, depending on the type of work you are completing, you may also be required to insert a separate title page (stating the full title of the work, the author's full name, and the academic institution it is being submitted to), a contents page (listing all the different sections included in the work), and an abstract page (containing a brief explanation of the aims and objectives of the work, its methodology, and its findings).

Creating In-Text Citations in APA Format

At this stage, it does not matter whether you are referencing a book, journal article, edited volume or online source, as all of these are referenced the same way in-text. The general system for referencing is as follows:

Author(s) (Year, Page); or

(Author(s), Year, Page).

This will be discussed in more detail below, with specific examples provided as to exactly how different types of citations should be presented.

Referencing a Source with One Author

In cases where the author's name is already stated as part of your sentence, you should simply insert the publication year of the author's work you are referring to, directly after the author's name, in brackets.

For example:

Author (Year) noted that…

If you have not already stated the author's name as part of your sentence, you should insert this, followed by the publication date of the work, at the end of the sentence in which you refer to it, or at an appropriate break in the sentence. It should appear in brackets, and the two pieces of information should be separated by a comma.

For example:

> There are some critics that have disputed these findings (Author, Year).

If it is not possible to supply a year of publication – as, in some cases, this information is not given (usually, in regards to online sources) – then you should insert 'n.d.' in place of the date.

For example:

> There are some critics that have disputed these findings (Author, n.d.).
>
> Author (n.d.) stated that…

Quoting a Source with One Author

If you've already given the author's name as part of your sentence, you need to supply both the publication year and the page number of the quote in brackets, directly after the name of the author. A comma should be used to separate the year and the page number, followed by 'p.' or 'pp.' (depending on whether or not the quote spans more than one page).

For example:

> Author (Year, p.00) stated that '(quote inserted here)'…

If not, you will need to state the author's name, the publication year, and the page number in brackets, at the end of the sentence in which you refer to it. A comma should separate the author from the year, and a comma followed by either 'p.' or 'pp.' (depending on whether the quote spans more than one page) should be used to separate the year and the page number.

For example:

> Some critics have argued that '(quote goes here)' (Author, Year, pp. 00-99).

If it is not possible to supply a publication date and page number and/or range – as, in some cases, this information is not given (for instance, digital books rarely have page numbers assigned, and if you're quoting from a film, you will not have a page number either) – then you should insert 'n.d.' in place of the date, and 'n.p.' in place of the page number(s).

For example:

> Author (n.d., n.p.) stated that '(quote inserted here)'…

> Some critics have argued that '(quote goes here)' (Author, n.d., n.p.).

Referencing a Source with Multiple Authors

In the case of a source with two authors, you should simply insert the publication year of the authors' directly afterwards, in brackets, if you've already given the names of the authors in your sentence.

For example:

> Author 1 and Author 2 (Year) argued that…

If not, you'll need to supply both the authors' surnames, along with the publication date of their work, in brackets. The information should be separated by a comma.

For example:

> These findings were confirmed by other studies (Author 1 & Author 2, Year).

If it is not possible to supply a year of publication, then you should insert 'n.d.' in place of the date.

For example:

> There are some critics that have disputed these findings (Author 1 & Author 2, n.d.).

When referencing a source that has three or more authors, you should insert the publication year of the authors' work directly after their names, in brackets, if you have already named them as part of your sentence. It is customary to abbreviate the authors' names to just the first author, followed by the phrase 'et. al.', after the first citation.

For example:

> Author 1, Author 2 and Author 3 (Year) argued that…
>
> Author 1 et al. (Year) also noted that…

Again, if it is not possible to supply a year of publication, then you should insert 'n.d.' in place of the date.

For example:

> There are some critics that have disputed these findings (Author 1, Author 2 & Author 3, n.d.).
>
> Author 1 et al. (n.d.) also noted that…

Quoting a Source with Multiple Authors

When quoting a source with two authors, both the publication year and the page number should be supplied in brackets, directly after the names of the authors, if these are already a part of your sentence. A comma should be used to separate the year and the page number, followed by 'p.' or 'pp.' (depending on whether or not the quote spans more than one page).

For example:

> Author 1 and Author 2 (Year, p.00) advised that '(quote goes here)'.
>
> Author 1 and Author 2 (Year, pp.00-99) argued that '(quote goes here)'.

If you have not already supplied the two authors' names, these should both be inserted in brackets at the end of the sentence, along with the publication date of their work, and the page number the quote appears on.

For example:

> Some critics have noted that '(quote goes here)' (Author 1 & Author 2, Year, pp.00-99).

If it is not possible to supply a publication date and page number and/or range – as, in some cases, this information is not given (for instance, digital books rarely have page numbers assigned) – then you should insert 'n.d.' in place of the date, and 'n.p.' in place of the page number(s).

For example:

> Author 1 and Author 2 (n.d., n.p.) stated that '(quote inserted here)'...

When quoting a source that has three or more authors, the publication year and the page number should be supplied in brackets, directly after the names of the authors, preceded by the denotation 'p.' or 'pp.' (depending on whether or not the quote spans more than one page), if you are named as part of your sentence.

Again, it is customary to abbreviate the authors' names to just the first author, followed by the phrase 'et. al.', after the first citation.

For example:

> Author 1, Author 2, Author 3 and Author 4 (Year, pp.00-99) argued that...
>
> Author 1 et al. (Year, p.00) also noted that...

If it is not possible to supply a publication date and page number and/or range, then you should insert 'n.d.' in place of the date, and 'n.p.' in place of the page number(s).

For example:

> Author 1, Author 2 and Author 3 (n.d., n.p.) stated that '(quote inserted here)'…
>
> Author 1 et al. (n.d., n.p.) also argued that '(quote inserted here)'…

Referencing a Source Without an Identified Author

In cases where the source you are referring to has no named author(s), you should cite these using the first few words of the reference entry (which is usually the title although, in some cases, using the organisation/department name is appropriate).

If the material you are citing is taken from an article, a chapter taken from a book, or a web page, you should present this information in quotation marks.

For example:

> This article suggested that there is evidence to support this theory ("Article Name", Year).

However, if you are citing a book, brochure, periodical or report, you should italicise this information.

For example:

> The report offered a number of recommendations
> for alleviating this issue (*Report Name*, Year).

If it is not possible to supply a year of publication, then you
should insert 'n.d.' in place of the date.

For example:

> The brochure offers a number of options for the
> consumer to consider (*Brochure Name*, n.d.).

Quoting a Source Without an Identified Author

Again, in cases where the source you are quoting has no
named author(s), you should cite the first few words of the
reference entry instead, followed by the year of publication
and the page number(s).

If the material you are citing is taken from an article, a
chapter taken from a book, or a web page, you should
present this information in quotation marks.

For example:

This article suggested that '(quote inserted here)' ("Article Name", Year, p.00).

In this article, the argument is posed that '(quote inserted here)' ("Article Name", Year, pp.00-99).

However, if you are citing a book, brochure, periodical or report, you should italicise this information.

For example:

The report stated that '(quote inserted here)' (*Report Name*, Year, pp.00-99).

If it is not possible to supply a publication date and page number and/or range, then you should insert 'n.d.' in place of the date, and 'n.p.' in place of the page number(s).

For example:

In the brochure, it is stated that '(quote inserted here)' (*Brochure Name*, n.d., n.p.).

This article suggested that '(quote inserted here)' ("Article Name", n.d., n.p.).

Referencing Multiple Sources

Sometimes, you may wish to attribute more than one source to certain statements in your work.

In cases where the names of all the authors you are referring to have already been stated as a part of your sentence, you should simply insert the publication year of each author's work you are referring to, directly after the author's name, in brackets.

For example:

> Studies by Author 1 (Year), Author 2 (Year), and Authors 3 & 4 (Year) have shown that…

If you have not already stated the authors' names, you should supply each of these in alphabetical order, followed by the publication date of the work in chronological order (i.e. earliest to latest), at the end of the sentence in which you refer to it, or at an appropriate break in the sentence. It should appear in brackets, and each piece of information should be separated by a semi-colon.

For example:

> Various critics (Author 1, Year 1, Year 2; Author 2, Year; Authors 3 & 4, Year) have argued that…

> There are many (Author 1 & Author 2, Year; Author 2, Year; Author 3, Year 1, Year 2, Year 3) who have disputed this…

If it is not possible to supply a year of publication for some or all of these sources, then you should insert 'n.d.' in place of the date wherever necessary.

For example:

> There are some critics that have disputed these findings (Author 1, n.d.; Authors 2 & 3, Year 1, Year 2, n.d.).

Quoting Multiple Sources

In instances where you need to incorporate a quotation into a statement containing multiple references, and the name of the author you are quoting has been stated as part of the sentence, you should supply the publication year and the page number of each quotation in brackets, directly after the name(s) of the author(s), preceded by the denotation 'p.' or 'pp.' (depending on whether or not the quote spans more than one page).

All other citations should be listed in alphabetical order, followed by the publication date of the work in chronological order (i.e. earliest to latest), at the end of the sentence, or at an appropriate break in the statement.

For example:

> Whereas Author 1 (Year, p.00) stated that '(quotation inserted here)', there are many other critics that have disputed this (Author 2, Year; Authors 3 & 4, Year, Author 5, Year).

In cases where authors' names are not stated as part of the sentence, the name of the author(s) should be inserted in brackets along with the year of publication and page number(s), directly after the quotation in each instance, or, if this is not possible, at an appropriate break in the sentence.

For example:

> Whereas some critics have argued that '(quotation inserted here)' (Author 1, Year, pp.00-99), others

have disputed this assertion, and have stated that '(quotation inserted here)' (Authors 2 & 3, Year, p.00).

If it is not possible to supply a publication date and page number and/or range, then you should insert 'n.d.' in place of the date, and 'n.p.' in place of the page number(s) wherever necessary.

For example:

Whereas Author 1 (n.d., n.p.) stated that '(quotation inserted here)', there are many other critics that have disputed this (Author 2, Year; Authors 3 & 4, Year, Author 5, Year), and have argued that '(quotation inserted here)' (Author 5, Year, p.00).

Creating a Bibliography in APA Format

As noted in the 'General Requirements' section, you will be expected to supply a full bibliography containing details of all your citations with every piece of work that you produce. This should be supplied at the end of the work, on a separate page or pages (depending on the length).

All entries should have a hanging indent, meaning all but the first line of each entry should be indented, and should be listed in alphabetical order (by the surname of the author, or by the surname of the first named author, if there are multiple contributors).

In general, references should contain the author name(s), publication date/year, the title of the source, page ranges, and the publication information (such as the place of publication and name of the publisher, the website address, or the volume/issue number).

As with the in-text citations, if it is not possible to supply a year of publication or page range for some sources, then you should insert 'n.d.' in place of the date, and 'n.p.' in place of the page number(s), wherever necessary.

This will be discussed in more detail below, with specific examples provided as to exactly how different types of citations should be presented.

Referencing a Printed Book

In cases where the book has only one author, you should start by listing the author's name (supplying the surname and initials, separated by a comma) and the year of publication (which should be supplied in brackets), before supplying the title of the book (in italics). Then, you should denote the place of publication (the city (and state), rather than the country) and the publisher's name, separating this information with a colon.

For example:

Author, A.A. (Year) *Title of Book*. Place: Publisher.

If you are quoting a book that has multiple authors, you should list each of the authors in turn (providing the surnames and initials, separated by commas), followed by the year of publication (in brackets), the title of the book (in italics), and the place of publication and publisher's name.

For example:

> Author 1, A.A., Author 2, B., & Author 3, C.D.
> (Year) *Title of Book.* Place: Publisher.

> Author 1, A. & Author 2, B. (Year) *Title of Book.*
> Place: Publisher.

If you have a reprinted or later edition of the book and wish to denote this, this should be inserted after the title of the book, in brackets.

For example:

> Author 1, A.A., Author 2, B., & Author 3, C.D.
> (Year) *Title of Book* (2nd edition). Place:
> Publisher.

If you need to denote any further information – such as if the text is a translation, the name(s) of the translator(s) – this should be supplied after the title of the book, in brackets, followed by the phrase 'Trans.'.

For example:

> Author 1, A.A., Author 2, B., & Author 3, C.D.
> (Year) *Title of Book* (E.E. Translator,
> Trans.). Place: Publisher.

Referencing an Online Book

In cases where the book you are citing has been taken from an online source, you should list each of the authors in turn (providing the surnames and initials, separated by commas), followed by the year of publication (in brackets), the title of the book (in italics), as you would with a printed edition.

However, instead of supplying the place of publication and publishers name, you instead need to provide the web address that you used to obtain the book. This should be supplied in full, and preceded by the statement 'Retrieved from:'.

For example:

> Author, A.A. (Year) *Title of Book*. Retrieved from: <web address inserted here>

> Author 1, A.A., Author 2, B., & Author 3, C.D. (Year) *Title of Book*. Retrieved from: <web address inserted here>

If it is not possible to supply a year of publication for some or all of these online book sources, then you should insert 'n.d.' in place of the date wherever necessary.

For example:

> Author, A.A. (n.d.) *Title of Book*. Retrieved from:
> <web address inserted here>

> Author 1, A.A., Author 2, B., & Author 3, C.D.
> (n.d.) *Title of Book*. Retrieved from: <web
> address inserted here>

Referencing a Section or Chapter of a Printed Edited Volume

If you need to supply a citation for a titled section or chapter which has been taken from a larger, edited volume, you need to supply both the names of the chapter or section's author(s), followed by the title of the chapter.

Then, you should supply the names of the editors of the text. This should be preceded by the word 'In'., and followed by '(Ed.)' or '(Eds.)', depending on whether there is more than one editor or not. Please note that editors' names should be listed in a different format to the authors' names – they should appear with initials first, followed by the surname, rather than the other way round.

After this information, you need to provide the name of the book (in italics), and the page range of the section or chapter (in brackets). Finally, you should denote the location of the book's publication, and the name of the publisher (separated by a colon).

For example:

> Author 1, A.A. (Year). Title of Chapter/Section. In A. A. Editor (Ed.), *Title of Book* (pp.00-99). Place: Publisher.

> Author 1, A.A., & Author 2, B.B. (Year). Title of Chapter/Section. In A. A. Editor 1 & B. B. Editor 2 (Eds.), *Title of Book* (3rd edition) (pp.00-99). Place: Publisher.

In cases where the section or chapter has no specified author, you should supply the editor(s) name(s), in the author name format (i.e. surname first, then the initials), followed by '(Ed.)' or (Eds.)', depending on the number of editors, and the year of publication. Then, proceed to supply the title of the chapter, the title of the book (in italics), and the place of publication and publisher.

For example:

> Author 1, A.A., & Author 2, B. (Eds.) (Year) Title of Chapter/Section. In *Title of Book* (pp.00-99). Place: Publisher.

If the edited volume forms part of a collection or series, you should additionally specify to which volume you are referring – insert this information directly before the page range, inside the brackets.

For example:

> Author 1, A.A., & Author 2, B. (Eds.) (Year) Title of Chapter/Section. In *Title of Book* (Vol. X, pp.00-99). Place: Publisher.

Referencing a Section or Chapter of an Online Edited Volume

In cases where the chapter or section you are citing has been taken from a book you have sourced online, you should list each of the authors in turn (providing the surnames and initials, separated by commas), followed by the year of publication (in brackets), the name of the chapter or section, the names of the editor(s), and the title of the book (in italics), just as you would with a printed edition.

However, instead of supplying the place of publication and publishers name, you instead need to provide the web address that you used to obtain the book. This should be supplied in full, and preceded by the statement 'Retrieved from:'.

Additionally, in place of the page range, you should denote the chapter or section number (if this is supplied). If not, omit this denotation completely.

For example:

> Author 1, A.A., & Author 2, B. (Year). Title of Chapter. In *Title of Book* (Chapter No.). Retrieved from: <web address inserted here>

> Author, A.A., (Year) (Ed.). Title of Section. In *Title of Book* (Section No.). Retrieved from <web address inserted here>

> Author 1, A.A., & Author 2, B. (Year) (Eds.). Title of Chapter/ Section. In *Title of Book*. Retrieved from <web address inserted here>

Referencing a Printed Journal Article

When accessing journal articles, you will find that in addition to the usual details (author names, publication date, title, etc.), there are other pieces of information which you will have to supply in order to reference the article properly. This includes the name of the journal, the volume number and, in some instances, the issue number. Additionally, in some cases, the article will have been assigned a unique DOI number. DOI numbers (Digital Object Identifiers) are unique alphanumeric combinations assigned to individual articles, and act as a sort of barcode, allowing the article being cited to be easily located.

Whenever the DOI number is supplied, you will need to include this in your reference, at the very end – after the name of the author, the year of publication (in brackets), the name of the article, the name of the journal (in italics), the volume number, the issue number where applicable (in brackets), and page range (preceded by either 'p.' or 'pp.').

For example:

> Author, A.A. (Year) Title of Article. *Title of Journal.* 1(2), pp.00-99.
> DOI: 10.1234/ABCDE56789.

> Author 1, A.A., Author 2, B. & Author 3, C.D. (Year) Title of Article. *Title of Journal.* 5, pp.00-99. DOI: 10.1234/ABCDE56789.

In cases where a DOI number has not been supplied, you should follow the same conventions, omitting this final piece of data, but including all other relevant information, such as the author name(s), date of publication, title of the article and journal, the volume and issue numbers, and the page range.

For example:

> Author, A.A. (Year) Title of Article. *Title of Journal.* 1(2), pp.00-99.

> Author 1, A.A., Author 2, B. & Author 3, C.D. (Year) Title of Article. *Title of Journal.* 5, pp.00-99.

Referencing an Online Journal Article

Again, the exact citation required depends on whether or not a DOI number has been supplied for the article you are referring to.

If you have a DOI number for the article, then you should begin by supplying name of the author, the year of publication (in brackets), and the name of the article, followed by the name of the journal (in italics), the volume number, and the issue number where applicable (in brackets). You should then supply the DOI number – in this case, it is not necessary to also supply the website address, as the DOI number will allow the article to easily be located.

For example:

> Author, A.A. (Year) Title of Article. *Title of Journal.* 1(2). DOI: 10.1234/ABCDE56789.
>
> Author 1, A.A., Author 2, B. & Author 3, C.D. (Year) Title of Article. *Title of Journal.* 5. DOI: 10.1234/ABCDE56789.

However, if a DOI number is not available, then you should instead provide the web address that you used to obtain the article. This should be supplied in full, and preceded by the statement 'Retrieved from:'.

For example:

> Author, A.A. (Year) Title of Article. *Title of Journal.* 1(2). Retrieved from: <web address inserted here>

Author 1, A.A., Author 2, B. & Author 3, C.D.
(Year) Title of Article. *Title of Journal.* 5.
Retrieved from: <web address inserted
here>

Referencing a Printed Newspaper Article

The formatting conventions for citing newspaper articles
differ slightly from journal articles, in that instead of
simply supplying the year of publication, you are expected
to advise the exact date, in the format Year, Month Day (in
brackets).

For example: (2005, May 24).

Volume numbers and issue numbers are therefore not
required (as newspapers are issued daily), although you still
need to state the name of the publication (i.e. the
newspaper) as part of your citation.

For example:

Author, A.A. (Year, Month Day) Title of Article.
Title of Newspaper, pp.00-99.

Author 1, A.A., Author 2, B. & Author 3, C.D.
(Year, Month Day) Title of Article. *Title of
Newspaper*, p.00.

Referencing an Online Newspaper Article

In cases where you are referring to an online newspaper article, you should still state the author(s) name(s), followed by the exact date of publication (Year, Month Day, in brackets), the title of the article, and the name of the newspaper. However, you are then required to supply the full web address of the article preceded by the statement 'Retrieved from:', instead of any page number(s).

For example:

> Author, A.A. (Year, Month Day) Title of Article. *Title of Newspaper,* Retrieved from: <web address inserted here>

> Author 1, A.A., Author 2, B. & Author 3, C.D. (Year, Month Day) Title of Article. *Title of Newspaper*. Retrieved from: <web address inserted here>

Referencing a Printed Report or Data Set File

The requirements for citing reports created by government agencies, corporations, market research companies and large organisations differ from other citation requirements, in that it is appropriate to supply the name of the department or company here as the 'author', rather than the name(s) of individual(s).

For instance, when referencing a governmental report, you can refer to the department – e.g. Department of Health, or Education, or Foreign Affairs – first, followed by the year of the report's publication (in brackets), the title of the report (italicised), the place of publication, and the office responsible for its creation.

For example:

> Department Name (Year) *Title of Report.* Place: Office.

Similarly, when referring to reports created by corporate organisations (such as the annual reports produced by large companies), you can cite the name of the company, followed by the full date of publication of the report, the location of company headquarters, and the office responsible (if provided).

For example:

> Company Name (Year, Month Day) *Title of Report.* Place: Office.

In the case of data sets, you should replace the name of the office with the name of the author/compiler, if known.

Referencing an Online Report or Data Set File

In instances where the report or data set file has been accessed online, you should still advise the company name and full date of publication (if known), along with the title of the report.

However, you will need to supply the full web address used to access the report, instead of the place of publication, in the case of online sources like these.

For example:

> Company Name (Year, Month Day) *Title of Report.*
> Retrieved from: <web address inserted
> here>

> Department Name (Year) *Title of Report.* Retrieved
> from: <web address inserted here>

> Company Name (Year) *Title of Data Set or Survey.*
> Retrieved from: <web address inserted
> here>

If you wish you refer to a particular section or chapter within a report or data set, this information should be inserted directly before the title of the report.

For example:

> Company Name (Year) Title of Section/Chapter. In *Title of Report* (Section or Chapter No.) Retrieved from: <web address inserted here>

In cases where no date has not been supplied, it will be sufficient to use 'n.d.' to signal a lack of information – however, usually reports of this kind are dated in some way, and so you should be able to supply this information relatively easily.

Referencing a Dissertation or Thesis

If you wish to refer to another individual's dissertation or thesis paper, you should supply the name of the author, the year it was written, and the title. This should then be followed by the name of the institution, followed by the location of that establishment.

For example:

> Author, A.A. (Year). *Title of Dissertation*. Name of Institution: Location.

Referencing a Source Without a Named Author

If a source has no named author (this is rare, but does occasionally happen with online sources), then you should start the reference with the name of the article, webpage, periodical or report. This should then be followed by the date of publication (in brackets), and any publication information you have.

In cases where the source you are citing is an article, a chapter taken from a book, or a web page, you should present the title of the section as plain text (i.e. not in italics).

For example:

> Title of Article (Year) Retrieved from: <web address inserted here>

> Title of Chapter (Year) In *Title of Book*. Retrieved from: <web address inserted here>

However, if you are citing a brochure, periodical or report, you should italicise this information.

For example:

> *Title of Book* (Year) Retrieved from: <web address inserted here>

Title of Brochure (Year) Retrieved from: <web address inserted here>

If it is not possible to supply a publication date, then you should insert 'n.d.' in place of this.

For example:

Title of Article (n.d.) Retrieved from: <web address inserted here>

Title of Brochure (n.d.) Retrieved from: <web address inserted here>

Referencing Visual Material

When referencing audio or visual material, the 'author' is the creator, director, writer and/or producer (whichever is appropriate for the format to which you refer).

So, for instance, when referencing a film, you would supply the name of the director (the format Surname, Initials), followed by the denotation '(Dir.)', and/or the producer ('(Prod.)'). You would then need to advise when the film was made (in brackets), followed by the title of the film (in italics), the location of the studio in which it was made, and the name of that studio.

For example:

> Director, D. (Dir.) (Year) *Title of Film.* Place:
>   Studio

> Director, D. (Dir.), & Producer, P.P. (Prod.) (Year)
>   *Title of Film.* Place: Studio

If you need to refer to a television series, or a particular episode in that series, you would credit the writer and the director first, followed by the year that the programme aired on television. Then, you need to provide the title of the episode, the producer's name, and the title of the series (in italics). Finally, you should advise where it was filmed, and the name of the distributor or studio responsible for making the show.

For example:

> Writer, W. (Writer), & Director, D.D. (Dir.). (Year).
>   Title of Episode. In P. Producer (Prod.),
>   *Title of Series.* Place: Distributor/Studio.

If you wish to refer to a specific broadcast on television, such as an edition of the news, you should reference the producer of the broadcast, rather than anyone featured in the transmission (such as the newscaster). You will also need to supply the exact date the programme was aired, the place it was recorded, and the name of the broadcaster.

For example:

> Producer, P. (Prod.). (Year, Month Day). *Title of Programme*. Place: Broadcaster.

About Joanne M. Weselby

Joanne M. Weselby (1985-) was born in Sutton in Ashfield, England and grew up a stone's throw from Sherwood Forest.

As an adult, she went on to obtain a first class BA (Hons) in English Literature and Creative Writing from Nottingham Trent University in 2012, and was awarded both the Five Leaves Prize and the Pat McLernon Prize for outstanding academic achievements in her chosen field.

She now works freelance as a writer, academic researcher and copyeditor, and has written a number of successful books.

Books by Joanne M. Weselby

- ❖ 'First Class English Essays: A Collection of Short Essays'

- ❖ 'Citations Made Simple: A Guide to Easy Referencing', Vols. I-IV

- ❖ 'Never Too Late: A Mature Student's Guide to Going to University'

Success Stories?

If, after reading this book, you've found it to be helpful, why not let myself and others know about it by posting a review?

Alternatively, visit my Fan Page on Facebook at: https://www.facebook.com/jmweselby

Like, share, and leave me a comment – I'd be delighted to hear from you!

Made in the USA
Charleston, SC
13 August 2015